CW01639196

To Micheal;

hope these poems inspire
you to live your life
to its ultimate and cherish
every moment

So glad I found you

Lauren

Happy Valentine . xxx

The Gift...

If only you knew

THE GIFT *if only you knew*

Published by Simone Segal

Print Services
Guangzhou Dongyang Color Printing Co.,Ltd
No.12/23 Guangtang West Rd,
Tangdong, Dong Pu,Tianhe
Guangzhou, China, 510665

Originally Printed by MPG Biddles ltd
24 rollesby Road
Hardwick Industrial Estate
King's lynn, Norfolk
PE30 4LS, UK

ISBN: 978-0-9567143-0-5

Dedicated to you.

May all your wishes and dreams come true!

Love Simone Segal

Content

Thank You

Acknowledgements

With the warmest gratitude I would like to thank all these amazing people who took me on this incredible journey of wisdom and gave me the knowledge to create a happy, harmonious and successful way of living, and inspired me to write life changing poetry to inspire others. For all their wisdom, I would like to thank the great Earl Nightingale, 'The Strangest Secret', Charles Haanel, 'The Master key System', Wallace Wattles, 'The Science of Getting Rich', Waldo Emerson, 'The New Thought Movement' of the mid 1800s. Lynn Grabhorn, 'Excuse Me, Your Life Is Waiting', Rhonda Byrne, 'The Secret', and Bob Proctor, on his teachings of 'The Science Of Getting Rich' and 'The Secret'. I would like to say a big thank you to Ian Carr, graphic and media designer, for his superb creativity, on the layout and design of *THE GIFT,* and Richard Pinner for editing.

I would also like to thank with all my heart Machi, my partner, for his total love, guidance, encouragement and support. You are my rock, I love you! I would like to thank my dear friend Catherine Pasqualina Reynolds for all her love, support and encouragement, my darling angels my children, James Segal and Molly Segal, you both make me so proud, I love you! And all the love and support from my family, thank you all so much!

The Gift

This book is based on a concept that has been around for thousands of years. This idea, simply put, states that your thoughts and your feelings create your future, otherwise known as 'the law of attraction'. This idea was first presented to the western world in the early part of the 19th century by Waldo Emerson, and has since been gradually seeping into the world's consciousness. In the past hundred years, several best sellers including 'Think and Grow Rich', 'Master Key System', 'Science of Getting Rich', have all been based on this idea. Also 'The Secret' by Rhonda Byrne.

It was after studying these materials, and listening to the great Earl Nightingale, 'The Strangest Secret,' I became aware that living by this incredible concept, all my thoughts, feelings, and life, were changing for the better. Most of us like to hang around in our comfort zone, "negativity", it's easy there, just sink into ourselves and watch how others live the high life. We are happy to watch them, with no dreams, no faith in ourselves, or even our own lives.

This book is intended to, and will, change your life for the better. It all depends on how much you want to change. All you need is the desire, the belief, and to act according to the poems.

The Gift comprises of over fifty poems written in a witty, funny and easily understood format. It presents all the core aspects of the idea, visualisation, state of mind, thoughts and feelings, etc. In a step by step guide, each poem carefully explains these concepts and shows you how to achieve a successful, happy and harmonious life. Before each poem there will be a word or two from me, and a famous quote.

The way we think is the way we feel, worry and fear draw us to everything in life we hope to avoid, *THE GIFT* shows you how to obtain a healthy mind and therefore a healthy body, and the ability to reach desires and goals, ultimately happiness, health and prosperity!

Simone Segal

THE GIFT

In 1956 Earl Nightingale wrote and recorded a message called 'The Strangest Secret'. Today, over 50 years and millions of copies later his message "We become what we think about," is still a leading source of life changing inspiration!

Earl Nightingale changed my life! And now, I hope to change yours!

We Become What We Think About!

Earl Nightingale

THE GIFT

The Gift is the answer of a bright new dawn
The law of attraction in poetry form
These poems guide you to a life of success
They are simple instructions, one can easily digest
I live by the law and my life is so sweet
I would love to share this inspirational treat
What I think about I bring about, It's incredibly true
It's all in the *The Gift* about dreams that come true
We all need hope, and now is the time
The key to success, a changing of minds
When you take this on trust, what you are about to read
It will show you how, in life to succeed.
The theory has been around for thousands of years
But been kept a secret, so it appears
Now it's out, of this there is no doubt
I would like to tell you what it's all about.
What you are thinking, and how you feel
Is creating your future, It's called the law of attraction
And on this subject, I have been very well tutored
Life seems to be full of highs and lows

We all need a shield for the knocks and the blows
Controlled thoughts, and controlled feelings
Will grant you your wishes, and all you are dreaming.
Nothing comes easy, like learning to drive
But when you have mastered it well, your spirits alive
Nothing can stop you; you're well on your way
Confidence takes over, it's a brighter day
The same on this subject, in which that I write
For when you have mastered the concept
Your goals are in sight, you become what you think about
Sounds crazy but true, It's all in the poems
Written solely for you.
Read the rhymes, over and over
THE GIFT will be your 4 leaf clover
We all have the power, we all can succeed
Enjoy the poems
Take in what you read!

What I think about I bring about

CREATOR OF YOUR LIFE ARE YOU

In life, every thought and every feeling we have is creating our actions. Every action creates a reaction, and every reaction is your life, like a magnet you attract everything you think about towards you!

Everything Begins With An Idea

Earl Nightingale

CREATOR OF YOUR LIFE ARE YOU

Creator of your life are you
For what you think and feel comes true
You are a magnet and will attract
Any prolonged thought exact
You can have anything your heart desires
With shift of thought your life transpires
Exercise your mind to positive thoughts
Feeling good is what you ought
For if you can, for all it's worth
You realise you are living in Heaven On Earth!

YOUR SOUL YOUR SPIRIT

Your life is a play, your thoughts are your script, and you determine the outcome! If you don't like the direction your life is going, think how you would like it to be, and act upon those thoughts!

All you need is the plan, the road map, and the courage to press on to your destination!

Earl Nightingale

YOUR SOUL YOUR SPIRIT

When you think about it
Hey I'll give your thoughts a jerk
And tell you how I know
These things really work
Your soul and your spirit is really you
And your mind tells your body
What it should do
Your mind bears your thoughts
And they hold the key
I can't think for you
And you can't think for me
Your thoughts are your future
They were also your past
If you're not happy now
You can change them real fast
Your life is a play
Which you have to act
Your thoughts are your script

And will turn out exact
So think on, be happy
Change all the cast
Don't dwell on misfortunes
Let go of the past
For now is the time
In your thoughts you can mould
What you want in your life
To have and to hold
And from this day forward
Like you are to wed
Marry these thoughts
Inside your head
For you never knew
That you had this great gift
Create your own life
Give your thoughts a great Shift!

Act upon great thoughts

THINK POSITIVE

We all go through our everyday lives with so many thoughts, but when did you actually stop to think about what you are thinking about? Do you have any idea of the consequences of your thoughts? When you look back at your life and remember your greatest achievements, you were in a positively positive frame of mind, and how did that make you feel? Amazing I'm sure!

They can because they think they can!

Virgil

THINK POSITIVE

Think of what you think about
Have the courage to let go of doubt
Intend your life, as you wish it to be
Now hold those thoughts of what you see
Know they are your reality

Positive thoughts must persist
Overfill your mind with this
See yourself wonderfully free
Inspire thoughts of clarity
Think of how your life will be
Imagine happiness, health, prosperity
Visualise with strong intention
Enrich Your Life, It's Your Invention!

FOCUS WITH A PASSION

When you focus with a passion on all your desires, they will manifest! Alessandro Volta created the electric battery, what was he thinking? Everything in this entire universe was created by thought, what can you think of? We all have this great gift called imagination!

The big thing is that you know what you want!

Earl Nightingale

FOCUS WITH A PASSION

Focus with a passion
On what you want in life
Manifest your thoughts so great
Until you see the light
The light is where you're feeling
Ecstatic to the core
And everything you focus on
Will manifest for sure
We are creative beings
That's what our thoughts are for
You can think creatively
Let your visions soar
One person could change the world
That person could be you
You could think inspired thoughts
We all can this is true
Remember it was just one thought
That gave us electricity

If that one person did not think
How would our lives now be?
So focus with a passion
On all that you desire
Manifest your thoughts so great
AND SEE YOUR LIFE TRANSPIRE!!

We are creative beings

BY WAY OF THINKING

The way we think is the way we live, we can change the direction we are walking, we can also change the direction of our thoughts and our lives.

We are still masters of our fate. We are still captains of our souls.

Winston Churchill

BY WAY OF THINKING

I don't know how I lived before,
But every day was a chore,
I know now, by way of thinking
Shifts you into way of linking
Your thoughts to life with only joy no strife
Endless abundance, wealth and health
Ditch the thought of woe is me and sorrows
Create your future and happy tomorrows
Think all is well with the world and you
Feel the good in all you do
By great thoughts and wonderful feelings
Your life will have a whole new meaning
Bring on great thoughts this very hour
Feel the joys of your power
For in you is your crcator
Believe it now don't wait till later
Visualise what you want for you
As a science and fact it will come TRUE!!

GRATITUDE

When you are truly grateful, how do you feel? Live your life full of gratitude, and always feel great! This puts you in a wonderful positive vibrational place of feeling good!

The mind moves in the direction of our currently dominant thoughts, we are at our very best, and we are happiest, when we are fully engaged in work we enjoy on the journey toward the goal we've established for ourselves. It gives meaning to our time off and comfort to sleep. It makes everything else in life so wonderful, so worthwhile!

Earl Nightingale

GRATITUDE

Gratitude is a wonderful act
Realising you're grateful as a matter of fact
Attracting all you're grateful for
Thankful to your very core
Indicates where you are at
Thankful people thank you back
Universal love for all
Dreams that all come true
Express your life with gratitude, thank you, thank you, THANK YOU!!

FERTILE MIND

Our thoughts that we sow, are the fruits of our future!

What we plant in our subconscious mind and nourish with repetition and emotion will one day become a reality!

Earl Nightingale

FERTILE MIND

Your mind is like a fertile land
What you sow, so shall ye reap
You have two seeds to choose from
Which one will you keep?
The first is the seed of failure
The second the seed of success
Which one will you plant?
That will flourish at it's best
Your fertile mind, like the land
Does not really care
Either seed you plant
Will grow with fruits to bear
You have the choice, which seed to plant
Remember what you ought
When you have planted that very seed
You will be living off the fruits of your thoughts.

IT'S ALL WITHIN YOUR MIND

You are a thinking centre, sculpting your future with every thought! All you need is the determination and will to search for your happiness!

To find what you seek on the road to life, the best proverb of all is that which says; "leave no stone unturned"

Edward Bulwer Lytton

IT'S ALL WITHIN YOUR MIND

Your life is not within your hands
It's all within your mind
You are a thinking centre
Who is creating all your plans
Sculpt your future better
What you focus on is real
Push forward all creative thoughts
And then see how you feel
Feeling great is the key
To open all the doors
A little bit of discipline
Will wash away your flaws
For whomever has determination
You will gain the skill
And change your thoughts
From bad to good
With your very will
It's not an easy task I know

When you are full of grief
It requires power
For you to have belief
All you see in life today
Was created from a thought
From this very poem you're reading now
To everything you've bought
You can think of happiness now
Remember it's you who has the power
Control your life, by your thoughts and your feelings
Really this life has a whole new meaning
Hold onto this and don't despair
Amazing thoughts are in the air
When you're in the zone of positive thinking
Your dreams will all come true,
You know, life is really a ball
When you know, that you know
That you really know
THAT YOU CAN HAVE IT ALL!!!

Feeling great is the key

WHEN YOU

When you can master the concept of changing your thoughts of doubts and fears, and gain faith to all your desires and expectations, you will obtain the key to a happy, harmonious, healthy life!

Our environment, the world in which we live and work, is a mirror of our attitudes and expectations!

Earl Nightingale

WHEN YOU

When you think you can't, that's the time you can
When you are full of hate, that's the time to love
When you are raged with anger, that's the time to be cheerful
When you want to cry, that's the time to laugh
When you are faced with a nightmare, that's the time to dream
When you are sick, that's the time to feel well
When you are sad, that's the time to be happy
When you feel bad, that's the time to feel good
When you have nothing, that's the time to feel abundance
When you are fearful, that's the time for courage
When you feel weak, that's the time to be strong
When you have doubt, that's the time to believe
When you can master this concept, that's the time to live

A CLARITY OF VISION

When you can visualise that you already have all your wishes and desires, you will be attracting them towards you with great speed!

Picture yourself in your mind's eye having already achieved this goal. See yourself doing the things you'll be doing when you've reached your goal!

Earl Nightingale

A CLARITY OF VISION

A clarity of vision
Exactly, what is it that you dream
Feel as though you already have and live it
As strange as that might seem
Write it down on paper
All that you desire
Read it every morning
And at night when you retire
A clarity of vision
Exactly, what is it that you dream
Feel as though you already have and live it
It's strange but do believe
Feel as though you already have and live it
The key to success, a fact!
The law of attraction, a magnet
What you're feeling, you will attract
The wise men of all times
Have absolutely agreed

It takes clarity of vision
To know exactly all your dreams
When you feel like you already have and live them
YOUR GOALS WILL BE ACHIEVED!

What is it that you dream?

THE LAW OF ATTRACTION

We all know about the law of gravity, but do we know about the law of attraction? Some of the greatest teachers in history have said that the law of attraction is the most powerful law in our universe, every thought we have is a creation, the law does not care whether it's a good thought or a bad thought, whatever we are thinking we are attracting! Think of yourself as a magnet! Think and feel with all your belief that you already have all you wish for, and with absolute certainty you will attract it!

Everywhere man blames nature and fate, yet his fate is mostly but the echo of his character and passions, his mistakes and weaknesses!

Democritus

THE LAW OF ATTRACTION

Look at you, look at me, look at a rock, look at a tree
To look further than the surface, you would need a microscope
And if you were to look so deep, you would need the mind to cope
When you look through a microscope, it is a scientific fact
We all are the same, you, me, the rock, the tree
Made up of vibrational energy
Everything in this universe
Is made of cells, molecules and atoms
Split the atom and what do you see
The highest form of energy
The same as you, me, the rock, the tree
We are all moving at different vibrational paces
Positive and negative energy
Fills all time, minds and spaces
There are laws of this world, like the law of gravity
You know that it works, undoubtedly
There is also the law of attraction
Which is as exact as it is real
Your vibrational energy will attract to you
EVERYTHING YOU THINK AND FEEL!!!

ATTITUDE WITH STYLE

To have confidence is to have attitude with style! When you believe in something, and you know that you know you will succeed, you cannot fail! When you do everything in your daily life to the best of your ability, confidence will shine out with the greatest ATTITUDE WITH STYLE!

People are always blaming their circumstances for what they are. The people who get on in this world are they who get up and look for circumstances they want, and, if they can't find them, make them!

George Bernard Shaw

ATTITUDE WITH STYLE

Positive and negative energy
Pulls you strongly either way
Which do you choose to flow with?
To start you off each day
Each one has the power
To take you oh so far
Which of them do you choose?
To show you who you are
You have the power in you
To stand up and be strong
You do not have to fall down
When everything goes wrong
It's just the way you think my dear
It's just the way you flow
It's oh so easy to go down
Stop now and just say no!
Your thoughts are reality
Not always what you see

Good or bad, you have the choice
Which one will it be?
The more you flow on upwards
The higher you will climb
Fill yourself with positive thoughts
And always you'll be fine
Such an interesting game to play
And will only take a while
And when you've mastered it well my friend
You'll have great confidence, and that is,
ATTITUDE WITH STYLE!!!!!

You have the power in you

WILLPOWER

I'm sure at sometime in your life you have used willpower to reach a particular goal, when you reached that goal, do you remember how you felt? Amazing! That's how using willpower makes you feel, Amazing! We all have the will, and we all have the power, use it, and always feel amazing!

The difference between a successful person and others is not a lack of strength, not a lack of knowledge, but rather a lack in will!!

Vince Lombardi

WILLPOWER

If you do something half-heartedly
The results will turn out the same
If you're not being the best you can be
You have only yourself to blame
Everybody has willpower
Dig deep, I am not wrong
And when you find it hallelujah!
Now you can be strong
All you need now is a goal
To reach where you should be
And when you're there, you'll be so glad
That you are now in the 5% minority
This 5% I speak about
Are the people who become a success
They are the ones who had goals
And put their will to the test
They are the ones who never quit

And always did their best.

Have a goal, use your willpower

Yes, you have it in you

Be your best and never quit

AND YOU'LL BE SUCCESSFUL TOO!!!!!

All you need is a goal

DECISIONS

A great decision acted upon is a great step to your future!

Progress is impossible without change, and those who cannot change their minds cannot change anything!

George Bernard Shaw

DECISIONS

To make a decision, you have to decide
Don't take too long, life quickly goes by
When you have decided, act very prompt
For it is your decision, to go for your wants
It's you who decides which direction you take
It's all your decisions, in life you must make
So decide what to do, see with great vision
Create a wonderful life; it's up to you, YOUR DECISION!!!!

ONE HUNDRED MEN

When you put a 100% of effort into all you do, you cannot fail!

If you think you can, you can, and if you think you can't, you're right

Mary Kay Ash

ONE HUNDRED MEN

One hundred men aged 25
All with a glint in their eye
All wanting to be a success
So they thought they would give it a try
When they reached their 65th year
It became evidently clear
Only 5 men made it
Reached the grade
A few had jobs, and were being paid
The rest were living off the state
And asked the question why?
The five men looked back at them
And this was their reply
We had goals and inspiration
We had courage and determination
We used awareness, let our minds soar
We had faith to get out of bed for
We never quit, and we never stopped

We never doubted, we reached the top
We had desire and did our best
We used all our skills and nothing less
And that's why we are, A Great Success!

Never doubt,
reach to the top

THESE POEMS

Open the doors to a new way of thinking, create your life 'consciously' instead of 'unconsciously' Know your direction in life instead of just arriving there in shock!

All you have to do is know where you're going. The answers will come to you of their own accord!!

Earl Nightingale

THESE POEMS

These poems are doors
Which I have given you keys
To open them wide
And live all your dreams
Grasp all the words
Take them all in
You create your own life
From your spirit within
What you think is what you'll attract
It's an absolute science, as a matter of fact!

BRIM YOUR MIND'S CUP

Ban every fear and doubt, overfill your mind to the brim with positive thoughts, and know in your mind's eye you can't possibly fail!

The thing always happens that you really believe in; and the belief in a thing makes it happen

Frank Lloyd Wright

BRIM YOUR MIND'S CUP

Up and down, high and low
Feeling good, feeling bad, your energy flow
Where are you going, do you know?
You have the power, you have the control
To steer your thoughts and feelings, to reach all your goals
This is the way, the law of attraction
Your thoughts and your feelings, are your life in action
What you think about, you bring about
The choice is all yours, it's you who creates
Only you open doors
Visualise exactly all your dreams, don't be coy
The health, the love, the wealth, and the joy
Take time to do this every day
Feel like your wishes arc flying your way
Believe in your thoughts, and not what you see
Positive attitude is a state you must be
Ban every fear, ban every doubt
Create in your mind, a negative drought

Form a habit of awareness; be conscious of your mind
Control your own thoughts, and there's where you'll find
The power within you, to master your mind
Your dreams coming true
All your great thoughts
You have attracted to you
It's hard at first; you will think you're at war
Fighting off demons, of your thoughts from before
You have to step out, of your comfort zone
It's positive attitude that will create your own throne
To be king and creator, of your very own life
Think and feel your way to success
A life without strife
When your mind is full of woe is me and sorrow
That's exactly what you're creating for your tomorrow
But if positive thoughts brim your mind's cup
Scientifically proven
That's the way up!

Feel like your wishes are flying your way

MAINTENANCE

Every day we realise that we have to maintain absolutely everything, our bodies, our homes, our cars, etc, but the most important thing to maintain are our minds. Stress is the number one cause of illness from dandruff to cancer. All we need to do is be aware of what we are thinking about, making sure we are in a positive frame of mind, and to love thinking in this way!

Thinking is the hardest work there is, which is the probable reason why so few people engage in it!

Henry Ford

MAINTENANCE

You maintain your house to keep it clean
You maintain your car so it's pristine
You maintain your physique, by keeping slim
You maintain your muscles in the gym
But the most important maintenance of all
Is to maintain your mind with positive thoughts.

CREATOR

Remember, everything you are thinking about during your day is creating your tomorrow!

The best way to make your dreams come true is to wake up!

Paul Valery

CREATOR

Create your life by your thoughts and your feelings
Realise the power in you
Establish all the good in your dreaming
Attracting it all back to you
Think positively and don't you sway
Original thoughts are on the way
Remember you create your every single thoughtful day!!!

WHAT YOU SEE IN THE MIRROR

Set yourself free from negative thoughts, not everything is as it seems. Your world will be as you create it in your mind. Take it on trust, when you believe in your dreams, you will live them!

The future belongs to those who believe in the beauty of their dreams!

Eleanor Roosevelt

WHAT YOU SEE IN THE MIRROR

Your mind your thoughts, they are you
What you see in a mirror is not so true!
It's what you are thinking
That makes you feel good
Think about this, you really should
It's how you feel, what people perceive
It's your vibrational energy, do believe
If you're on a low, that's where you'll go
And all that surrounds you are on the same flow
I know you have been there many a time
What brought you back, was it your mind?
Yes it was your mind for sure
You had had enough in that state
Only you had thc powcr to opcn the gate
And set yourself free
To come back to reality
Feeling happy is a natural state to be
If only you realise the power in you

A prolonged thought, will come true
But must be held with passion and feeling
Take this on trust, because seeing is believing,
When you feel wonderful, and life is great
The world around you will flow in this state
But to keep it there and not fall back
You must Never ever think of lack
This is something you've never done before
Cast every bad thought out the door
Every moment of every day
Positive thoughts must be in play
It's hard to do at first I know
You must keep battling on
It's when you're thinking positive thoughts
Nothing can go wrong
You will slip at times, but that's OK
If you get back on track straight away
For that is where you will find
The creation of all your desires
HELD WITHIN YOUR MIND!!!!!

When you feel wonderful and life is great, the world around you will flow in this state.

BE HAPPY

When you can be happy before you are happy, you will become happy!

Always keep that happy attitude. Pretend that you are holding a beautiful fragrant bouquet

Earl Nightingale

BE HAPPY

Be happy just for happy's sake
Be happy for no reason
Be happy just for happy's sake
Pretend it's happy season
Be happy just for happy's sake
Happy you must be
Be happy just for happy's sake
And happy you will be
Be happy just for happy's sake
Believe me it is true
When you're happy just for happy's sake
IT CREATES A HAPPY YOU!!!!!!!

FEEL IT

When you are feeling great your vibrational energy is attracting all your dreams towards you. Hold great feelings always! When you are not thinking positively you don't feel good. The moment you realise this, as hard as it might be, change your thoughts!

Hold fast to dreams, for if dreams die, life is a broken winged bird that cannot fly!

Langston Hughes

FEEL IT

It's important to think
But more so to *feel*
You need the connection
To make your thoughts real
If you made a wish, and your wish had come true
How would that *feel?*
If it happened to you
You would *feel* ecstatic, no maybes, if's or buts
You would FEEL excited from your stomach to your guts.
Now hold it right there!
Wish something for you
Feel with strong intention
That your wish has just come true!
For that is the place where you should be
Feeling ecstatic internally!
Your thoughts are your wishes, of all you desire
But your *feelings* of passion
Make your life transpire!

So come on, get wishing
Don't leave it too late
Remember to *feel* excited
Or your wishes will *disintegrate!*

Wish something for you

I AM WELL

When you are sick, try with all your will to imagine yourself healthy and strong. Remember, you attract all your thoughts, so picture yourself well. The mind is more powerful than you could ever imagine! You have the power in you, believe!

The surest way not to fail is to determine to succeed!

Richard Brinsley Sheridan

I AM WELL

I am healthy, I am well
My body repairs naturally every cell
I am constantly aware, that I am feeling great
And will never ever contemplate feeling any other way
My healing thoughts are here to stay
For what I think is so real, my body adjusts to how I feel
I feel fantastic every waking hour, I am so grateful for this power
It's mind over matter, this is true
So always think of a healthy you!!

I AM THE SOURCE

Intend your life as you wish it to be, all your desires, constantly think about them, act on your thoughts, and follow your intuition, GO FOR IT!

Keep steadily before you the fact that all success depends at last upon yourself!

Theodore T. Hunger

I AM THE SOURCE

I am the source, the spirit of thee
I create with intention, what my life will be
I intend to be happy
I intend to have health
I intend to be loved
I intend to have wealth
And all these things I intend for me
I intend for the world, with intentional glee!

INDIVIDUALITY

Never follow the crowd, they are usually unable to think for themselves and blindly follow others. Have faith in yourself, only you know the right direction which is right for you!

The man who makes a success of an important venture never waits for the crowd. He strikes out for himself. It takes nerve, it takes a great lot of grit; but the man that succeeds has both. Anyone can fail. The public admires the man who has enough confidence in himself to take a chance. These chances are the main things after all. The man who tries to succeed must expect to be criticized. Nothing important was ever done but the greater number consulted previously doubted the possibility. Success is the accomplishment of that which most people think can't be done!

C. V. White

INDIVIDUALITY

To regain individuality, is an absolute necessity
Most people follow the crowd; it's a very unfortunate game
We follow each other in the masses, and all end up with the same
And then we ask the question why this is so?
The answer to this is, we have no goals!
We follow like sheep, where others go
We do not think for ourselves you know
All we need is inspiration; the life we lead is our own creation
Let us conform no longer
Let's be different, let's be stronger
Let us stand out from the crowd
Be individual and shout out loud!
I have to just think positively
Think of what I want for me
Regain my individuality
For then will come my clarity
On what I choose my life to be!

HAPPINESS

Do all the things you love to do, even if it seems selfish! How can you make anyone else happy if you are not happy?

Happiness depends more on the inward disposition of mind than on outward circumstances.

Benjamin Franklin

HAPPINESS

Happiness is state of mind
Admiration for all mankind
Positive thoughts and passionate feelings
Present to you a life with meaning
Inspired dreams that will come true
Never sad or feeling blue
Escape to where you will find
Serenity and peace of mind
Success and joy are on the way, and happiness is here to stay!!!

HA HA, HE HE

It's always good to laugh. It's better than any doctor's prescription! Go see a funny film, see the funny side of things.

Most folks are about as happy as they make up their minds to be!

Abraham Lincoln

HA HA, HE HE

Ha ha, he he
Ha ha, he he
Ha ha, ha ha, he he
He he, he he, ha ha, he he
LAUGH, IT'S GOOD FOR THEE!!!!

PAY THE PRICE

Thoughts and willpower are not a big price to pay, in fact they are a very small price to pay, but the rewards are enormous!

Happy are those who dream dreams and are ready to pay the price to make them come true!

Leon J. Suenens

PAY THE PRICE

This is how I'm going to be
Successful in what's best for me
I'm going to think in a positive way
My thoughts and willpower is the price I'll pay
I'm going to think of what I want to do
Then have the courage to see it through
I will always remember and never forget
To act on great thoughts, and have no regrets
I will not entertain any negative thoughts
For I now have the skills in which to abort
Anything that's not in line with me
For I am content and happy you see
I love myself and feel strong this way
And happy am I, every single day
To have success you need to pay the price
Think positively to be precise
It can't be worse than feeling blue
And a failure in all you do
So pay the price be happy be strong
WHEN YOU PAY THE PRICE, YOU CAN NOT GO WRONG!!!!

I BLINKED AND HE WAS THERE

When you believe in love and are so full of love, think love, feel love, love will turn up, you attracted it!

Believe that you have it, and you have it!!

Latin Proverb

I BLINKED AND HE WAS THERE

I asked the universe for a man so sweet
Nectar could not compare
With such belief and heart of love
I blinked and he was there
My life is full of love and joy
Words can't express my bliss
His eternal love for me
Intoxicates my lips
This love we have, I wish upon
The whole wide world to share
I wish you all to blink
And love would be right there!

LOVE

If it's love you need, start with loving yourself. You are your own best friend truly. Love yourself like the greatest love you have ever felt for anyone, fill yourself with so much love that you overflow with love for all, and all will fall in love with you!

A loving heart is the truest wisdom

Charles Dickens

LOVE

Love yourself and all you see
Overflow with love for thee
Visualise your love story
Experience love in all its glory!

RELAX

Stop Worrying about everything, it just makes matters worse, be calm, take time out, do something that relaxes you, your thoughts will become much clearer when you are calm.

Let no feeling of discouragement prey upon you, and in the end you are sure to succeed!

Abraham Lincoln

RELAX

Relax, be calm
Be quiet, be still
Relax, be patient
Let go, and chill
Relax yourself and you will find
Peace and comfort, so well defined
You now feel content, refreshed and fine
Your stress has gone, left far behind!

THE BEST THINGS IN LIFE

Inside us all there is love, gratitude, attitude, positivity, and confidence. It does not cost a penny to use any of these amazing gifts you hold. When used, an abundance of all your desires will be flying towards you like a magnet!

You must be the change you wish to see in the world!

Mahatma Ghandi

THE BEST THINGS IN LIFE

The best things in life, it's true, are for free
How much does it cost, to love infinitely?
How much does it cost, for overwhelming gratitude?
How much does it cost, for inspiring attitude?
How much will it be, to think positively?
How much does it cost, to have confidence and stand tall?
It costs absolutely nothing! No, nothing at all!!!!!

YOUR DESTINY

All your thoughts, all your feelings, all your actions, are steering you towards your destiny!

You are what your deep driving desire is. As your desire is, so is your will. As your will is, so is your deed, as your deed is, so is your destiny!

Brihadaranyaka Upanishad 1V4.5

YOUR DESTINY

Do you know your destiny?
Is it written anywhere you can see?
No, your destiny lies in your mind
And is solely up to you to find
Your destiny is the creation of all your thoughts
What you are thinking steers your way
Controlling your each and every day
What you think about, you bring about
It's as simple as can be
So be careful what you think about
Because that's *your destiny!*

TAKE TIME AND NOTICE

Take time out of your busy life, and take time to notice the beautiful world around you!

Learn to enjoy every minute of your life. Be happy now. Don't wait for something outside of yourself to make you happy in the future. Think how really precious is the time you have to spend, whether it's at work or with your family. Every minute should be enjoyed and savoured!

Earl Nightingale

TAKE TIME AND NOTICE

Sweet velvet chocolate taste
A warm night breeze across your face
A new born baby's very first smile
Children playing all the while
Birds flying in the sky
Wishing wells where waters lie
Oceans deep and oh so blue
Brilliant sunshine gleaming through
The moon, the stars
They shine so bright
Turns the black night sky to light
A twinkle in one's eye of joy
A smile that offers love
The smell of flowers in full bloom
So fragrant they are, they fill the room
Be still, and feel your own heart beat
Celebrate your life
Take time to notice
The World Is Wonderful And Bright!

SMILE

Just by smiling can change your attitude towards life! Do the things that make you feel happy, hold onto this thought with a smile!

Get into line what you will find to be a deep personal interest, something you really enjoy spending twelve to fifteen hours a day working at, and the rest of the time thinking about!

Earl Nightingale

SMILE

Smile, it can change your thoughts
Go on, give me a grin
The more you stretch it across your face
Your spirit uplifts from within
You start to feel so good inside
You feel happy on this smiling ride
Just as long as you keep on smiling
It's not such an effort to do
Hang on in the smiling ride
Smile, you'll be a happier you!

THE BEST

Do not stand in the way of your own opportunities. When you do the very best at everything you do, you can only receive the best results!

Most of the shadows of this life are caused by our standing in our own sunshine!

Ralph Waldo Emerson

THE BEST

Think your best

Say your best

Do your best

Be your best

Have the best!

OUT OF YOUR MIND

When you have control over your mind, you have control over your life!

We can let circumstances rule us, or we can take charge and rule our lives from within!

Earl Nightingale

OUT OF YOUR MIND

Are you out of your mind?
Not happy with your lot?
Are you out of your mind?
Are all your dreams forgot?
Do you think you are good for nothing
And there is nothing you can do?
Well get back in your mind
'cause I have got news for you
This is your life, it's you who creates
Get back in your mind
It's never too late
When you are back in your mind
You have total control
Of every direction, you want to go
When you are back in your mind
You can have all you dream
So get back in your mind

Give those cobwebs a clean
Now you are back, your thoughts will transpire
If you act on those thoughts
You will have all you desire
This is your life; give it your best shot
Do not be lazy, live your dreams, have the lot
So get back in your mind, Take total control
Go live your dreams
YOUR MIND IS NOW WHOLE!

You can have all you dream

IT'S REAL

There is nothing, or no one in this world that can tell what you are thinking except the law of attraction. More than that, it delivers everything you are thinking about to you! How will you use this information? Be aware of what you are thinking about. Remember, good or bad thoughts you will attract!

Nothing can stop the man with the right mental attitude from achieving his goal; nothing on earth can help the man with the wrong mental attitude!

Thomas Jefferson

IT'S REAL

The law of gravity is not to be frowned
If you fall out a tree, you'll come tumbling down
But the law of attraction pulls every way
Good and bad energy, finding a place for it's stay
So be aware what you think, be aware how you feel
What you are attracting, will latch on for real
Think and feel happy, that's what you'll attract
Do not feel sad, or you'll be asking for that
The law of gravity can make you fall down
But the law of attraction can turn your life around
You are what you think, you are how you feel
Live by this law, understand it, IT'S REAL!!!!!

YOU ATTRACTED READING THIS

For some reason, you attracted this book to you, whether you believe it or not! That reason is the law of attraction!

Your imagination is your preview of life's coming attractions!!

Albert Einstien

YOU ATTRACTED READING THIS

As luck would have it
But luck is not the word
You attracted reading this
Although it sounds absurd
I have a message for you
I would like to plant this seed
Believe this information
That you are about to read.
Love attracts love
Hate attracts hate
Peace attracts peace
Happiness attracts happiness.
I could go on, it’s an endless list
What you are attracting will persist
So be aware of all that you think
You know what I mean
Nudge nudge, wink wink

OBSESSION

See yourself Well! Many people have cured themselves with their mind's ability. Think health, feel health, attract HEALTH!!

Change your thoughts, and you change your world!

Norman Vincent Peale

OBSESSION

They say an obsession
Is not good for oneself
I beg to differ,
If it's an obsession for health
If you want to succeed
To be healthy and strong
See Yourself Well!
Be obsessed by your vision
You will never go wrong!!!

YOUR TOOLS

Every word written here is a gift that we all have. When you live your life putting these words into action, your life will be a great satisfaction!

Do not wait to strike till the iron is hot; but make it hot by striking!!!

William B. Yeats

YOUR TOOLS

These are your tools that you need to succeed
That is only, if you act upon all that you read
Mind, Think it
Imagination, Imagine it
Vision, Visualise it
Perception, Perceive it
Individual, be it
Love, Feel it
Gratitude, Have it
Memory, Memorise it
Intuition, Sense it
Confidence, Show it
Willpower, Use it
Control, Master it
Patience, Wait for it
Dreams, Wish it
Faith, Believe it

Life, Live it

You have all these gifts in you,

Only, and only, when you act upon these words, will your life turn around for you!

Believe

BE YOUR OWN BOSS

When you are doing a job you love to do, you have learnt it, and mastered it, there is only one person you can really count on, that's yourself. Nobody knows but you the best decisions to take but yourself, no one can get the job done like YOU!

First say to yourself what you would be; and then do what you have to do!

Epictetus

BE YOUR OWN BOSS

Be your own boss
Set your own rules
Your thoughts and your feelings
Give you the tools
Imagination can be fun or a bitch
Imagine you're poor
Or imagine you're rich
Imagination, what is it for?
It's for living your life
You are creator
So be your own boss
Discipline is not hard to swallow
It's just setting the rules
In which you must follow
Be the best you can be
In everything you do
Remember this is not for me
You're doing it for you

So be your own boss
And make all your choices
Listen to you
And not other voices
Your life you create
By your thoughts and your feelings
So be your own boss
AND DO ALL YOUR OWN DEALINGS!!!!

Make all your choices

INSPIRATION

Always listen to your inner you! Nobody knows better!

Do we not agree to call rapid thought and noble impulse by the name of inspiration?

George Eliot

INSPIRATION

If I could give inspiration to you
With these words, would be a dream come true
I have seen a light so bright it shines
Telling me to express these thoughts of mine
Love yourself without contempt
Love all around you, have no resent.
Be grateful for who you are
Positive thoughts will send you far
Never doubt and never fear
Always listen to your inner ear
Your inner ear is spirit you
Correctly telling you what to do
If I could give inspiration to you
You would know for sure
THESE WORDS ARE TRUE!!

POSITIVE THOUGHTS AND VISUALISATION

Your life revolves around your mind! What do you visualise?

The universe is change: our life is what our thoughts make it!

Marcus Aurelius

POSITIVE THOUGHTS AND VISUALISATION

Positive thoughts and visualisation
Will undoubtedly manifest your life's creation
What is essential for us to flower
Is to have the knowledge of our power
To have the courage to dare, to show our flare
The faith to do, and see it through
Perception, memory, reasoning, will
Use all these wisely and you'll gain the skill
To reach for your goals
And give your spirit a lift
Use attitude, it is a great asset
Understand, we are in a new era
A change for all mankind
This gift you're receiving is the knowledge
That your life revolves around your mind
What you're thinking you will attract
GOOD OR BAD, IT WILL COME RIGHT BACK!!!

OPEN DOOR

Open a new door, choose a new script! A new life's adventure!

Dream lofty dreams, and as you dream, so shall you become. Your vision is the promise of what you shall at last unveil!

John Ruskin

OPEN DOOR

I know myself, like never before
I have just walked through an open door
My feet still steady on the ground
A whole new world I have found.
It's rich in all, the greatest gift you see
Please come through and walk with me
We will only go where we will find
Reality is state of mind
What you are thinking is who you are
Walk on with me and you will go far
Have control; write the script of life in bliss
And forever only think of this.
Cast all bad thoughts away
Ban them on return
Go back to your script, feel the uplift
And your world will change before you
You will know who you are
What you want
AND THAT EVERYTHING IS FOR YOU!!

JUST WOKE UP

Wake up! And live a blissful life!!

Hope is the dream of a man awake

French Proverb

JUST WOKE UP

I have just woke up and I'm in heaven
Of this I tell you true
If you want to know how I got here
I have this message for you.
A constant state of bliss is needed
And only then have you succeeded
It's not easy, this is true
To have blissful thoughts when feeling blue
Master your thoughts, you take control
Think only bliss, you are on a roll
Keep it up, don't ever sway
And very soon will come that day
When you have woken up and are in heaven
For when you reach this very state
Elation you will feel
That constant state of bliss in you
Your bliss is now for real
Health, wealth, a blissful attitude
A wonderful life of love and joy
FULL OF BLISSFUL GRATITUDE!!!!

Use your habit every day

You must keep thinking in this way

Use your willpower, you have it in you

YOU WILL BE AMAZED AT WHAT 30 DAYS CAN DO!!!

Use your habit everyday

30 DAYS AFTER

How wonderful is life! Congratulations! Now you know what I'm talking about! It took great willpower I know, we all have it, but the difference is that you used it. Can you imagine what the world would be like if we all succeeded in the 30 day test? Spread the word!

You always pass failure on the way to success!

Mickey Rooney

30 DAYS AFTER

Congratulations! For your 30 day straight run
Watch what happens now my friend
Your life will be so much fun
The habit you formed some time ago
Thinking positive every day
You're going to realise now my friend
Negative thoughts have gone away
You worked so hard, it took great strength
You did not stop at any length
When negative thoughts came to say hi
You did kick them out with an outstanding goodbye
Now you will see that they hardly return
And when they do, you will be unconcerned
You have now built your mind to be courageously strong
You have mastered your mind, you can not go wrong
See how easy life will be, your mind is toned and you are free
To reach your goals, your destiny
This 30 day test, my friend is no fake
For you now have a habit, that's too hard to break!!!!

NEVER GO BACK

When you come to the realisation that your thoughts and feelings are creating your future, it's almost impossible to turn a blind eye to this fact, it works! You know what to do, you know how to think, you know how to feel, act upon these words, and your dreams become REAL!!!

If you won't be better tomorrow than you were today, then what do you need tomorrow for?

Rebbe Nachman of Bratslav

NEVER GO BACK

When you read these poems
Do you really take them in?
Or do they go in one ear
Then out the other again?
If you want a successful life
Please do take them in
Read them over and over
Until they have all sunk in
We are living in a new era
We are becoming aware of our minds
The way to success is now clearer
This is the greatest changing of our time
What you're thinking and how you feel
Will create your life, the truth for real
Once these poems have sunk in
You will definitely be on the right track
And if they really have sunk in
There will be no turning back

This book, The Gift, is my dedication to you
Live by its code, and you'll never feel blue
Thank you for reading, take care and God bless
I wish you all well, and the GREATEST SUCCESS!

Love Simone

Comments

IT'S ALL WITHIN YOUR MIND

Simone, your poems are like bright lights, and all the words like bulbs, emitting hope and life>>lovely write>>

James Fraser

PAY THE PRICE

Awesome write! I dream of success. I will often reread this one……

Nicole Sharon Brown

WHEN YOU

Very powerful indeed. Everyone must master their own lives like this. Very good message and I am looking forward to reading more…..

Kevin Elmore

YOUR SOUL YOUR SPIRIT

Easy flow…great message… it should be on a poster in a classroom!!!

Richard Bates

DECISIONS

So simple a truth, so profoundly expressed……..

William A Cleator

ATTITUDE WITH STYLE

Awesome uplifting write here, Simone!!!......

Sue Mason

WHAT YOU SEE IN THE MIRROR

Hi Simone, this poem is truly powerful medicine for the soul and I am amazed how you are able to convey these images within our minds….

Dean Masciarelli

I AM WELL

Beautiful and inspirational!........

Audrey Carey

THINK POSITIVE

Hi Simone, nice to meet you! I got such a kick out of this inspiring poem.
I Just know your words will touch the hearts of all your readers as
it did mine. Thanks
So much for sharing this amazing write with us,
take care love light truth…

Patricia Adams